The Body Book

An Owner's Guide to Fueling, Fixing, and Running the Most Important Machine You Own

SCHOLASTIC INC.
New York Toronto London Auckland Sydney
Mexico City New Delhi Hong Kong Buenos Aires

Illustrations
Jeff Moores

"Pumping Up" adapted from "Heart Thumping Workouts" from *Scholastic Choices,* January 1999. Copyright © 1999 by Scholastic Inc. All rights reserved.

"Stay Off the Bench" adapted from "10 Tips: How to Avoid Sports Injuries" by Jonathan Fox from *Scholastic Choices,* March 2000. Copyright © 2000 by Scholastic Inc. All rights reserved.

"Energy Boosters?" adapted from "Eating Right for Exercise" by Rachel Rivera from *Scholastic Choices,* March 2000. Copyright © 2000 by Scholastic Inc. All rights reserved.

"The Skinny on Fat" adapted from "Four Fat Rules" by Maura Christopher from *Science World,* January 22, 2001. Copyright © 2001 by Scholastic Inc. All rights reserved.

"There's Fat . . . And There's Fat" and "Quiz: Are You a Fool for Fat?" adapted from "Types of Fat" and "Just the Fats, Ma'am!" from *Science World,* January 22, 2001. Copyright © 2001 by Scholastic Inc. All rights reserved.

"A Killer Flu" adapted from "Silent Killer" by Alexandra Hanson-Harding from *Junior Scholastic,* February 21, 2000. Copyright © 2000 by Scholastic Inc. All rights reserved.

"Foods That Kill (Well, Sort Of . . .)" adapted from "Germ Warfare" by Chana Stiefel from *Scholastic Choices,* March 2001. Copyright © 2001 by Scholastic Inc. All rights reserved.

"Get Some Sleep" and "Dream On" by John DiConsiglio adapted from *Scholastic Choices,* February 2001. Copyright © 2001 by Scholastic Inc. All rights reserved.

"*Don't* Go for the Burn" adapted from "Heat Rays" by Chana Stiefel from *Scholastic Choices,* May 2001. Copyright © 2001 by Scholastic Inc. All rights reserved.

Contents

Introduction

Your body is like a machine. Take care of it and it runs well. Abuse it and it breaks down. You know the feeling. You've had the same cold since you were 13. You can't catch your breath after taking out the garbage. Getting out of bed feels like coming out of a coma.

Maybe you don't worry much about it. You can always start exercising, tomorrow . . . give up potato chips, tomorrow.

To a certain extent, you're right. Your body's young. It recovers fast. But the longer you wait, the harder it gets. Couch potatoes at age 16 are likely to be couch potatoes at 26, 36, and 46.

Besides, why not start now? Imagine what you could do with the extra energy. And if you're already an athlete, think of how much better you'll get.

So, read on. It's your body. Consider this book your owners' manual.

1 Exercise Your Heart

You're walking up the stairs on the way to class. A friend is spouting off about how girls shouldn't be allowed on boys' sports teams. You want to tell him to shut up. But by the time you can get a word in, you're at the third floor. You're so out of breath, you can't even talk. And you might as well forget about running around the soccer field.

What's going on? The last time you checked, you were young and healthy. So why are you gasping for air?

Chances are, you're out of shape. And you're not alone. Almost half of Americans between the ages of 12 and 21 don't get enough exercise. In fact, only two in 10 high school students are physically active for more than 20 minutes a day.

That means that a lot of teens are missing

out on the benefits of **aerobic exercise**. That's exercise that strengthens your heart—the most important muscle in your body. The better shape your heart's in, the better it can do its vital work of pumping oxygen-rich blood through your body. (To find out more about how your heart works, see "Pumping Up" on page 11.)

So what will getting your heart in shape do for you? First, there are the obvious things. You'll be able to run faster and longer. You'll recover quicker after getting out of breath. And you'll control your weight by burning calories faster. But there are also some benefits you probably wouldn't expect. People who get a lot of aerobic exercise tend to sleep better. They can control stress and depression better than couch potatoes.

Plus, if you exercise while you're young, you'll be glad later. Experts say what you're doing—or not doing—now can affect you for the rest of your life. Out-of-shape kids are likely to become heavy, out-of-shape adults. And they'll be more likely to have health problems. Inactive people have a higher risk of heart disease, **osteoporosis** (bone loss), and **diabetes**.

Fortunately, all it takes are 20 to 30 minutes of aerobics a day to help you stay in good health. Here are some tips for getting started.

- **Think long, slow workouts.** Your workout should make you breathe harder. Running, swimming, biking, and playing basketball or soccer are aerobic. Lifting weights is not.

- **Get your rate right.** During your workout, you should get your heart pumping at 60–80 percent of its maximum rate.

   Huh? Okay, to find your maximum rate,

subtract your age from 220. So, if you're 18, for example, your maximum heart rate would be 202 beats per minute. Your heartbeat should never, ever be faster than that.

Now, figure out what your rate should be during a workout. Multiply your maximum rate by 80 percent. That's as high as you should go in a workout. (In our example, that's 202 x .80 = 161 beats per minute.) Now multiply your maximum rate by 60 percent. That's as low as you should go in a workout. (In our example, that's 202 x .60 = 121 beats per minute.)

And how do you figure out your heart rate? First, find your **pulse** in your neck or wrist. Then count the number of beats in 15 seconds. Multiply by 4 and you've got your heart rate.

- **Warm up and cool down.** Start slowly so you get your heart rate up gradually. Too much stress on cold muscles can cause injuries. And don't stop suddenly while your heart is pumping blood like mad. That's a good way to bring on cramps or dizziness.

- **Don't burn out too fast.** You're not trying to set records in the 100-meter dash. Aerobics is all about endurance. The goal is to get to your target heart rate and maintain it for 20 to 30 minutes. If you get up too high too fast you won't be able to keep it up.

- **Be realistic.** Don't set your goals too high. Getting some aerobic exercise every day is a good idea. But you might be too busy to get to the gym or run. Instead, turn everyday activities into exercise. Walk a little faster on the way to school. On weekends, rake leaves at a quicker pace.

Pumping Up

How does your heart work, anyway?

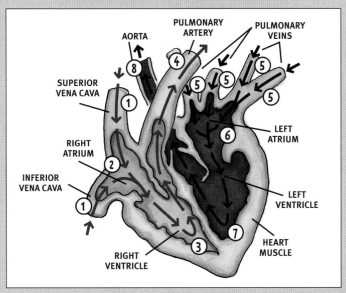

1. Blood from the body enters the heart from two large veins: the **inferior vena cava** and the **superior vena cava**.
2. The blood then accumulates in the **right atrium**.
3. Next, the blood passes into the **right ventricle**.
4. Then, the blood moves into the **pulmonary artery** to the lungs. In the lungs, blood receives oxygen.
5. The oxygen-rich blood then moves into the **pulmonary veins**. (There are two pulmonary veins from each lung.)
6. Next, the blood moves into the **left atrium**.
7. It then travels into the **left ventricle**.
8. The oxygen-rich blood is pumped back into the body through an artery called the **aorta**.

And how long does this process take? Sixty seconds!

Stay Off the Bench

Ten Ways To Avoid Sports Injuries

1. **Stretch.** Warm-up slowly and stretch before any sport or activity. Flexible, warmed-up muscles don't get injured as easily.

2. **Shape up.** Get in shape *before* you start playing a sport. Most injuries happen early in a season, before muscles are ready for the stress.

3. **Drink up.** Always drink plenty of water. Start drinking water before a game, practice, or workout. Continue drinking water *while* you're exercising. And do it whether you feel thirsty or not.

4. **Shell out for shoes.** Buy running shoes for running, basketball shoes for basketball—you get the idea. And replace worn-out pairs quickly. Good shoes won't just help your feet. They'll cushion your body, from your ankles to your neck.

5. **Respect pain.** Exercise can—and should—make your muscles sore at times. But if the pain doesn't go away, it's time to pay attention. That's your body's way of telling you it's injured. Get yourself checked out by a doctor or **physical therapist**. And slow down or stop until you heal.

6. **Sweat the small stuff.** Treat even minor injuries with care. Don't start working out again until you've healed completely.

7. **Ask questions.** If you're not sure how or when to exercise, ask a gym teacher, coach, or doctor. Or you can go to the library and ask a librarian to suggest books and web sites. (Just to get started, go to **www.about.com** and search for: exercise and beginning.)

8. **Keep your teeth.** If you play contact sports, wear a mouth guard. Sports like ice hockey, football, or rugby give dentists a lot of business.

9. **Rest.** With exercise, you can have too much of a good thing. Take at least one day a week off. Giving your muscles time to recover actually helps you get stronger.

10. **Eat right.** Think of your body as a luxury car: Don't fill it with cheap gas. Eat lots of **carbohydrates**, such as whole-grain breads. Fruits and vegetables are good, too. So is protein. You'll find protein in meat, eggs, fish, tofu, and nuts. But try to keep your fat intake low.

Energy Boosters?

**Will sports drinks and energy bars
get you to the big leagues?**

	Energy Bars
What they promise	A high-energy boost from carbohydrates. Most bars are packed with high-carb foods like oats and nuts.
Do they work?	Yes, but you can get the same result from food in your kitchen. And energy bars won't give you all the nutrients your body needs. So use them only when you absolutely can't have a real meal.
What you need	For energy, eat 60 to 90 minutes before exercise. Try a variety of foods high in carbohydrates and low in fat. A bagel (without too much cream cheese) will work. So will a bowl of cereal, or a handful of crackers. It's also important to eat after working out.
What you don't need	Some energy bars are high in sugar and fat. Anybody who is trying to lose weight should avoid these high-calorie bars.

Sports Drinks

A quick energy boost. They also say they'll keep you hydrated. (That means they'll keep plenty of water in your body.) And they say they'll restore the salt you lose during exercise.

Sports drinks are mostly water and carbohydrates, flavored with sugar and salt. Your body breaks down carbohydrates into **glucose**, which is a great energy source. So, these drinks can give athletes an extra burst of energy. They also replace salt and liquids. But you can get the same results by drinking juice mixed with water!

A 150-pound athlete can lose 6 cups of fluid in an hour of activity. If it's not replaced, you can get cramps or heat exhaustion. You should drink 10 to 14 ounces of fluid 1 to 2 hours before activity. (FYI: There are 8 ounces in a cup.) You should also drink 10 ounces immediately before exercise; 4 to 6 ounces every 15 minutes during exercise; 16 ounces after exercise.Try half water and half cranberry, orange, or grape juice.

Sports drinks have high sugar and calorie counts. If you are just tossing a Frisbee around, you could drink more calories than you burn.

2 The Skinny on Fat

A lot of people like the *idea* of eating well. But if you're like most, you don't think you have the time for it. So, you get chips and a soda from the vending machine for lunch. After school you pick up a packaged apple pie for a snack. You get home late and grab a ham sandwich for dinner.

What's the one thing these pick-up meals have in common? Fat—and lots of it. But before you sentence yourself to a life of steamed broccoli, get educated. Not *all* fat is bad. In fact, your body needs fat to function. So don't run from fat—rule it. These four rules will show you how.

Rule 1: You need *some* fat.

Fat isn't a four-letter word. It's a **nutrient**. That's a substance that helps your body function.

Fat is one of five important nutrients. The others are **proteins**, carbohydrates, **vitamins**, and **minerals**. Fats perform many jobs. They provide energy for sports and help your body absorb vitamins A, E, D, and K. These vitamins, in turn, help your blood clot. They also help absorb **calcium**, form red blood cells, and more. If your skin is glowing and your hair is glossy, you probably have fat to thank.

Rule 2: Not all fats are equal.

All fats have about 120 calories per teaspoon. But different fats affect your body in different ways. (See the chart "There's Fat . . . And There's Fat" on page 22 for more details.) The important thing to remember is this: All fats have some effect on **cholesterol** levels in the body. Cholesterol is produced in the liver. It helps the body produce Vitamin D and absorb fat. But too much of it clogs your arteries. That makes your heart work harder and can lead to heart disease.

Not all cholesterol is the same, either. LDL cholesterol is bad for you. It tends to catch along

artery walls and harden. HDL cholesterol, on the other hand, helps you stay healthy. It collects bad cholesterol and carries it back to the liver, where it can be broken down. So, the idea is to eat fats that increase the HDL in your blood stream and decrease the LDL. (Rule 4 and the chart will tell you how.)

Rule 3: Thirty percent or less.

You need fat. You just don't need a lot of it. That's because fat is packed with calories. There are 9 calories in a gram of fat. Compare that to protein or carbohydrates, which have 4 calories per gram. (There are about 14 grams of fat in a tablespoon.)

Too much fat can lead to clogged arteries, heart disease, and strokes. And these conditions can start when you're young. If you eat a lot of greasy food, ugly fatty streaks may already be building up in your arteries. Chances are you're putting on extra pounds. And carrying too much weight will sap your energy. Researchers also think fat may be linked to some cancers.

How much fat is okay? It should make up 30 percent or less of your daily calories. Here's a simple formula to help you figure this out: (your weight) x .45 = your target number of daily fat grams. Suppose you weigh 140 pounds. Just multiply 140 by .45. You'll find that you shouldn't eat more than 63 fat grams a day—maximum. And if you want to lose weight, you should eat a lot less.

Once you know this number, check out the labels on the food you eat. If you eat at fast-food restaurants, ask for the information at the counter. You can add up fat grams for a couple of days and see how you measure up. Or, you can use a short cut. Look for two numbers: total calories, and calories from fat. Divide the first number into the second. If the result is less than .30 (30 percent), you're headed for your target.

Rule 4: Substitute healthy fats for less healthy ones.

Remember, "good" fats are the ones that increase HDL and decrease LDL. They're called *mono-* and *polyunsaturated fats.* The "bad" fats are **saturated fats** and *trans-fatty acids*. Try to keep the good fats in and the bad fats out. Here are some tips:

- Use canola or olive oil when cooking. Skip the butter, margarine, or other oils.

- Pass up the snack foods that list hydrogenated oils in the top four ingredients. The word *hydrogenated* refers to a process that turns unsaturated fat into saturated fat.

- If you can't resist french fries, pick the smaller portion.

- Identify all the fats you add to food yourself. This probably includes butter, margarine, mayonnaise, and salad dressings. Cut the amounts you use in half.

- Try to eat more fish. Albacore tuna with low-fat mayonnaise is a good bet. Salmon is healthy, too.

There's Fat ... And There's Fat

What do different fats do, anyway?

	Main sources	Effects
SATURATED	• meat • dairy products, such as cheese and ice cream • palm and coconut oils	Negative. Raises the level of LDL (low-density lipid, or fat) cholesterol in your blood. LDL is the "bad" cholesterol. It sticks to artery walls and blocks the flow of blood.
MONOUNSATURATED	• olive oil • canola oil • avocados • nuts	Positive. Lowers LDL cholesterol blood levels. Raises the level of HDL (high-density lipid) cholesterol in your blood. HDL—the "good" cholesterol—helps the body get rid of LDL.
POLYUNSATURATED	• soybean oil • corn oil • safflower oil	Mixed. Lowers bad LDL levels, but also lowers good HDL levels. Some polyunsaturated fats—like safflower oil—might actually increase the risk of getting cancer.
TRANS-FATTY ACIDS	• stick margarine • vegetable shortening • commercial fried foods • packaged baked goods	Negative. Raises bad LDL levels and lowers good HDL levels. Increases heart disease risk.
OMEGA-3	• fish, particularly albacore tuna and salmon • walnuts	Positive. Protects against heart disease. Helps keep the heartbeat steady. Eases muscle aches by keeping swelling down. Helps protect against some tumors. Aids nerve cells in the brain. Might help depression and attention-deficit disorder.

Are You a Fool for Fat?

Take this quiz to find out if you're treating your heart right. Pick a number for each question. Then add up your total and check your score below.

How often do you eat . . .	seldom or never	1–2 times per week	3–5 times per week	almost daily
fried, deep-fried, or breaded foods?	1	2	3	4
whole milk, ice cream, or high-fat cheese?	1	2	3	4
baked goods (not fat free)?	1	2	3	4
fatty meats, such as bacon, sausage, cold cuts, and hot dogs?	1	2	3	4
hamburgers (not of lean meat)?	1	2	3	4
chips and other high-fat snack foods?	1	2	3	4
tuna or other fish?	4	3	2	1
food cooked in olive or canola oils versus another oil?	4	3	2	1
nuts or peanut butter?	4	3	2	1
soft or squeezable margarine?	4	3	2	1

Your Score

10-20: You're no fool. Just remember, you do need some fat in your diet.

21-24: Not bad. But try skipping a few doses of fries and chips.

25-40: You're a fool for fat. Time to get the grease out. Reread Rule 4.

3 Top-Ten Reasons Not to Smoke

Why, you might ask, does anyone need to be told—again—about the dangers of smoking? All you have to do is read a pack of cigarettes. It says right there that smoking can cause cancer. If you're pregnant, it can harm your baby. It can even kill you. Enough said, right?

Wrong. All you have to do is breathe the air outside your school. You know the message isn't getting through. The fact is that more than one in three high school students smoke. Maybe they forgot how to read. Maybe they think it won't hurt them because they're young. Maybe they think they'll quit tomorrow. Maybe they *like* gasping for air on the way to the second floor.

Or maybe they just need a few more details. So, here are the top-ten reasons not to smoke.

10. *You prefer white teeth to yellow.* Cigarettes have tar in them. That's the same dark, sticky stuff they use to make roads. When you inhale it, it turns your teeth yellow. Smoking can also make your gums recede and your teeth fall out.

9. *One of these days, you'd like to have healthy kids.* Smoking makes both men and women less fertile. It can also lead to impotence. And smoking while you're pregnant is an especially bad idea. It can cause miscarriage, birth defects, and premature delivery.

8. *You wouldn't normally choose to inhale rat poison, toilet-bowl cleaner, or dead-frog preserver.* And those are only a few of the things cigarettes have to offer. According to the American Lung Association, cigarette smoke contains more than 4,000 chemicals.

7. *There's not really any need to kill insects inside your lungs.* Nicotine is the main drug in cigarettes. Scientists call it an alkaloid. Plants produce alkaloids to fend off leaf-chewing bugs. So, tobacco that doesn't meet the standards for cigarettes is often used to make insecticides.

6. *Nicotine poisons your brain faster than a needle full of heroin.* Drugs injected into a vein take 14 seconds to get to the brain. Nicotine gets there from your lungs in eight seconds. If you injected nicotine, it could take just three cigarettes' worth to kill you.

5. *You'd rather not look old at 35.* Smoking destroys **elastin**, the stuff that keeps your skin smooth. It also shrinks blood vessels near your skin. That means skin cells get

less oxygen and moisture. The result: wrinkles, especially in women.

4. *For the most part, you enjoy breathing.* Cigarettes seriously cut your oxygen supply. As smokers puff away, some of the oxygen in their blood is actually replaced by carbon monoxide. That's the stuff that comes out of your car's tail pipe. Smoking also stunts the growth of your lungs. All of this means you'll never be as good at sports as you could be. Even climbing stairs can seem like a chore.

3. *Getting cancer isn't on your list of things to do before you die.* Approximately 170,000 Americans die of lung cancer every year. About 90 percent of them are dead because they smoked. If you smoke a pack a day, you are 20 times more likely to get lung cancer than non-smokers.

2. *You'd like your heart to keep working.* Smoking shrinks blood vessels and cuts the oxygen in your blood. So, your heart has to pump 10 to 25 more times each minute. Even then, it doesn't do its job well enough. Smokers get cold hands and feet because their circulation is bad. And they have more strokes and more heart attacks.

1. *You don't want to die.* That's what happens to nearly 400,000 smokers every year. That makes about 1,100 Americans who die of smoking-related diseases every day. Of today's young people in America, about five million could die early from smoking.

Who's Been Smoking?

Fewer adults are smoking, but teenage smoking is on the rise.

National Center for Health Statistics, National Health Interview Survey

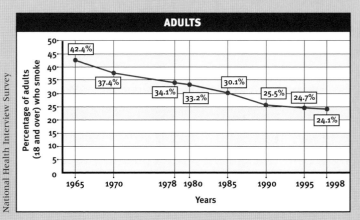

ADULTS

About one in four American adults still smokes. But that's a drop since 1965, when close to half were smokers.

University of Michigan, Institute for Social Research, Monitoring the Future Project

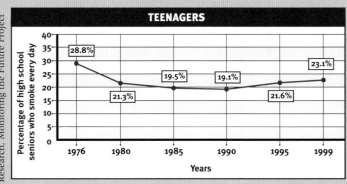

TEENAGERS

Since the early 1990s, cigarette smoking has been on the rise for American high-school seniors.

4 What's Bugging You: A Cold or the Flu?

We can cure heart disease. We can transplant kidneys and other organs. We can replace hips and knees. But we haven't figured out a cure for the common cold.

Every year Americans get one billion colds. Kids get six to eight of them a year. Adults average two to four. Colds account for 15 million lost workdays annually.

And then there's the flu. **Influenza** strikes 20 to 50 percent of Americans each winter. Many of those people are laid up with fevers for days.

Colds and flu are so common, you would think we'd know a lot about them. In fact, doctors don't know all that much. And the average cold sufferer knows even less. That's why we've been able to sum it up in just six pages.

So, what's the difference between a cold and the flu?

They're not easy to tell apart. Both are infections of the nose and throat. Both are caused by viruses. Colds tend to come on slowly. First you get a scratchy, sore throat. Then comes sneezing and a runny nose. Eventually it might settle into a mild cough. The symptoms can last from two days to a week.

The flu is more intense. All at once, you may get a headache, a dry cough, and chills. You're probably tired. Your back and legs ache. You could have a fever of up to 104 degrees. The fever lasts for two or three days. Then you get **nasal congestion** and a sore throat. You might be weak for days or even weeks.

How do you get a cold or the flu?

They're both transmitted through **mucus**. That's the stuff that comes out when you cough or sneeze. You can pick it up by shaking hands or touching doorknobs or rails. The germs make their way into your body when you touch your eyes, nose, or mouth. Or you can get sick simply by breathing. If someone has coughed or sneezed near you, the germs can hang in the air. Flu germs, for instance, last for three hours in the air.

Are they dangerous?

Yes and no. No one really has to worry too much about colds. They can lead to infections in your ear or sinuses. But those are usually easily treated with **antibiotics**.

For some people, the flu poses a much bigger problem. If your **immune system** is weak, the flu can give you **pneumonia**. Some 10,000 to 20,000 Americans die that way every year. Almost all of them, however, are elderly, newly born, or chronically ill. If you're young and healthy, you probably have nothing to fear except a few days of misery.

Can they be cured?

Not really. Of course, there are hundreds of cold and flu medicines at the drugstore. But they treat the symptoms, not the cause. They might stop your nose from running. Or they'll keep your fever down. But they won't make your cold go away. The best thing you can do is not get sick in the first place.

Okay, so how do I keep from getting sick?

The flu can sometimes be prevented with a **vaccine**. It works 70 to 90 percent of the time. Flu season goes from about December to March. The vaccine takes six to eight weeks to start working. So the best time to get it is mid-October. Ask your doctor or your school nurse. As for colds, wash your hands a lot, drink lots of fluids—and read "Cold Comfort" on page 35.

What about staying out of the cold or rain?

Colds and the flu do tend to hit in fall and winter. But it's not the weather's fault. The problem is that when it gets cold, people spend more time indoors. Everyone is locked up in close quarters. Germs have nowhere to go. And you become a sitting duck for viruses.

So, the chances are I'm going to get sick anyway. What do I do then?

The most important thing is to let your body heal itself. That means getting lots of rest. If you're tired, your immune system will be weak. It won't do a good job of fighting off the virus. Drinking lots of liquid and using a **vaporizer** can help, too.

Cold medicines are okay. They'll probably make you feel better and help you sleep, which is a good thing. Nasal sprays aren't a great idea. After a day or two they can actually make your congestion worse. You should also be cautious of aspirin as well. If you have the flu or chickenpox, it can lead to a rare—and dangerous—disease called Reye's syndrome.

Cold Comfort

**Here's how to avoid getting sick
in the first place.**

- **Wash up.** Your mother's right. You should wash your hands well and often. Flu germs can survive there for a half-hour. In that time, chances are you'll rub your eyes or scratch your nose. Next thing you know, you'll be in bed on a beautiful day.

  All it takes is 15 seconds of scrubbing. Use soap and warm water. And steer clear of antibacterial soaps. They kill good bacteria as well as bad.

- **Stay strong.** Viruses like weak and tired bodies. Sleep well, exercise a lot, and eat healthy food. Strong, well-rested bodies are much better at fighting germs.

- **Stay moist.** Drinking liquids and using a vaporizer can help. Dry **membranes** may actually be welcoming to viruses.

- **Stay away.** If you really can't afford to be sick, steer clear of people who are. At the very least, watch for sniffling people who cough without covering their mouths. And stay away from used tissues that haven't been thrown out.

A Killer Flu

In 1918, a deadly flu epidemic swept across the globe.

On April 21, 1919, Grace Keeney of Castile, New York, died from the flu. She was only 40, in the prime of life. And she left a family of eight children.

The Keeneys' tragedy was just one among millions that year. During 1918 and 1919, one of the worst epidemics in history swept across the globe. Approximately 50 million people died—of the flu.

This version of the flu—or influenza—was nicknamed "the Spanish flu" because one of the first outbreaks took place in Spain. It was 25 times more deadly than usual. It killed so many people that the average life span in the United States fell by 12 years. In 1917, it was 51. In 1918, it sank to 39.

It was a horrible and brutal illness. Typically, flu patients would complain of severe headaches and high fevers. Eventually, their faces would turn brownish-purple and their feet black from lack of oxygen. Eventually, they would drown in the liquid that filled their lungs.

The flu changed the routine of everyday life. Public meetings—at school, church, and other places—were canceled. The city of Tucson, Arizona, went even further. It barred anyone from appearing in public without a mask "covering both the nose and the mouth."

Still, no one knew how to stop the disease. The *American Journal of Public Health* simply told people to bury corpses quickly so the dead would not lie around too long. Eventually, the virus just ran its course. It killed the weak. And those left standing became immune to the disease.

Today we have vaccines that protect against the flu. But every year, new strains pop up. Most of them are not deadly. But scientists say that one could come again.

© Hulton Archive

Nurses care for victims of the flu in Lawrence, Massachusetts, in 1918. The fresh air was thought to speed patients' recovery.

5 Foods that Kill (Well, Sort Of . . .)

You can't see them, smell them, or taste them. But they're lurking everywhere. They're in the ground, on your hands, even floating in the air. They're **pathogens**—disease-causing germs—that make their home on the food you eat. At meal time they can hitch a ride into your body and make you sick. One day you're biting into a juicy burger. The next day you're down with food poisoning. You're vomiting. Or maybe your stomach is cramping, and you've got diarrhea.

Each year, 76 million Americans suffer from food-borne illnesses. How do they get sick? In many cases, germs get into our food from animal waste. Sometimes it happens as meat is getting processed. Animal intestines may not be separated well enough from the edible meat.

In other cases, manure in soil can get into

fresh fruits and vegetables. Even humans can cause a problem. People who don't wash their hands after going to the bathroom can easily contaminate food.

But there's no need to starve yourself. Most food in the United States is safe. And a small amount of germs won't make you sick. And even if you do get food poisoning, it usually lasts only a few days. In rare cases, it can put people in the hospital. Really bad cases can lead to death. So if you get sick after eating something, it can't hurt to see a doctor.

In the meantime, there are plenty of ways to keep food germs away. Here are a few common mistakes people make—and some simple rules for correcting them.

Rule 1: Food that can spoil needs to be stored in cold temperatures.

Mistake: At the start of the school day, you shove a turkey sandwich in your locker. At lunchtime, you decide to grab some fries with your friends. Later, you're hungry again. So you eat the turkey sandwich.

Problem: Lunch meats may contain small amounts of *Staphylococcus aureus* **bacteria**. A 40-degree refrigerator will keep the germ from growing. But a warm locker acts like a greenhouse. Germs grow like mad. And your sandwich gives you a stomachache, diarrhea, and vomiting.

Solution: When in doubt, throw it out. Never leave **perishable** foods out of the fridge for more than two hours. Watch out for lunch meats, tuna salad, and anything made with

mayonnaise. All these things need to stay cold. Store them in a cooler with an ice pack or in a refrigerator.

Rule 2: Cook all meat, poultry, and seafood thoroughly.

Mistake: You fire up the grill and throw on some burgers. After a few minutes, they're burned on the outside. They're still red and juicy on the inside. You pull them off and serve them up.

Problem: Any beef could contain *E. coli* bacteria. But ground meat has a greater chance of having germs. That's because it's been ground up with a lot of other meat. So it's especially important to cook ground meat all the way through.

Solution: Stick a meat thermometer in the burgers to tell when they're done. Cook ground beef to at least 160 degrees. Steaks should be cooked to 145 degrees. Poultry needs to be served at 180 degrees. Fish is done when it no longer has that glassy look on the inside.

Rule 3: Keep foods clean.

Mistake: The strawberries in the fridge look delicious. So, you reach in and grab a handful. Then you pop them in your mouth.

Problem: Fruits and vegetables can carry *E. coli, Salmonella, Shigella, hepatitis A,* and other germs. They get contaminated from farm

manure or bird droppings. Besides, you don't know who touched the produce at the supermarket. Who knows when they last washed their hands?

Solution: Wash all fruits and vegetables before you eat them.

Rule 4: Don't spread bacteria from raw meat and poultry to other surfaces.

Mistake: You decide to surprise your parents with a dinner for their anniversary. First you cut up some raw chicken on a cutting board. Then you use the same board and knife to make a salad.

Problem: Raw meat can contain bacteria like *Salmonella* and *Campylobacter.* You'll cook the germs out of the meat itself. But they're still thriving on the cutting board. Thanks to your salad, your parents could spend their anniversary in the bathroom!

Solution: Wash your hands in hot soapy water before and after touching food. Wash cutting boards, knives, and anything else that has touched raw meat.

Food for Thought

How smart are you when it comes to food safety? Take this quiz and see. You'll find some—but not all—of the answers in this chapter. When you're finished with the quiz, count how many questions you got right. Then check your score on page 47.

1. **Why are germs from hamburger meat more dangerous than germs from steak?**
   a. Hamburger has more fat in it.
   b. Bacteria can spread throughout the meat when it's ground.
   c. People cook hamburger less than steak.
   d. All of the above.

2. **When are hamburgers completely safe to eat?**
   a. When they are black on the outside.
   b. When they first come out of the refrigerator.
   c. Two hours after cooking.
   d. When the insides have been cooked to 160 degrees.

3. **What should you do with leftovers after a meal is cooked?**
   a. Throw them out.
   b. Let them cool down for 3–5 hours, then refrigerate.

c. Put them in the refrigerator as soon as possible.

d. Eat everything right away.

4. Which of these helps protect against germs when you're handling meat?

a. Wash your hands after handling raw meat.

b. Wash cutting boards in hot water and soap after every use.

c. Don't use a wood board for cutting meat.

d. All of the above.

5. Raw cookie dough is okay to eat if . . .

a. it's store-bought.

b. it's made without eggs.

c. it's made with **pasteurized** eggs.

d. All of the above.

6. Fruits and vegetables are probably fine to eat if they are . . .

a. washed thoroughly.

b. grown in your state.

c. grown in your own garden.

d. bought from a clean store.

7. **If a roast beef sandwich has been in your locker all day, you should . . .**
   a. throw it out.
   b. put it in the fridge for two hours before eating it.
   c. scrape the mayonnaise off and then eat it.
   d. give it to a friend.

8. **When washing dishes, it's best to . . .**
   a. let them soak for a long time in warm, soapy water.
   b. wash them within two hours of eating.
   c. dry them quickly after washing.
   d. All of the above.

9. **When thawing meat, you should not . . .**
   a. let it sit at room temperature.
   b. heat it in the microwave.
   c. let it sit in cold water.
   d. leave it in the refrigerator.

10. **After you buy meat, it should be eaten or frozen within . . .**
   a. one day.
   b. two days.
   c. five days.
   d. a week.

Answers

1. **b.** Bacteria collects on the surface of raw steak. As a result, the heat from cooking kills the germs easily. When the meat is ground, the germs work their way to the center, where they are harder to kill.

2. **d.** Stick a meat thermometer in the center of your burger. When it reads 160 degrees, eat up.

3. **c.** Get leftovers into the fridge within 2 hours of cooking. When you reheat, heat to 140 degrees or more.

4. **d.** Bacteria from raw meat doesn't die when it leaves the meat. It lives on your hands, on cutting boards, and on counters. Hot water and soap will take care of it.

5. **d.** Eggs can contain *Salmonella* bacteria. *Salmonella* causes a particularly bad kind of food poisoning. Pasteurized eggs are okay. And pre-made dough sold in stores has been pasteurized.

6. **a.** Fruits and vegetables can pick up bacteria from manure or bird droppings. Washing them well should make them safe to eat.

7. **a.** Bacteria has been growing on your sandwich all day. The roast beef could be contaminated. And if you put mayonnaise on the sandwich, that could be spoiled, too.

8. **b.** Food and warm water make a great home for bacteria. Letting dishes soak will only make germs grow. And it's best to let dishes air dry. That way bacteria won't be passed along with a towel.

9. **a.** Thawing meat at room temperature allows bacteria to grow.

10. **b.** Two days. Even in the refrigerator, bacteria will grow.

Your Score

8–10: Bravo. You're no friend to germs.

5–7: Not bad. A little more caution couldn't hurt.

1–4: You're skating on the edge. Warn your friends before inviting them for a barbeque.

6 Get Some Sleep

When it comes to sleep, many kids are like Liz Collins. The 17-year-old senior from McLean, Virginia, has trouble fitting it into her schedule. On a normal day, Liz drags herself out of bed at 6:30 A.M. She races to school for a 7:15 class. When the last bell rings at 2:30, she's still moving. She's got a meeting of the school newspaper. Then there's a deadline at the literary magazine. And she has to make it to winter track and crew practice. Some nights, she doesn't get home until 11. Then she'll do at least two hours of homework. When everything is done, she crawls into bed at 1 A.M. or later.

"I hate getting five hours of sleep," she says. "But I need all these activities to get into a good college. And more than that, I love sports. I love the newspaper. And I love taking challenging courses."

Experts have one piece of advice for people like Liz: Get some sleep! Eighty-five percent of all teens don't get enough shut-eye, according to the National Sleep Foundation (NSF). Teens average just over seven hours of sleep a night—two hours less than they need.

"I think most teens don't even know what it's like to be fully awake," says Dr. Mary Carskadon, a sleep researcher at Brown University. "It's like they are walking around with bad eyesight. When you get them back on a healthy sleep schedule, they are shocked at how clear everything is—and how good they feel."

Few people realize what a few zzz's can do for them. Sleep is like food for the brain. It lets cells repair themselves. The brain gets to process information it collected while it was awake. Muscles and organs rest and recover from a day's work. As a result, people who get enough sleep tend to be healthier, happier, and smarter. Studies even show that rested students get better grades than groggy ones.

On the other hand, skipping sleep won't just make you tired. It can be downright dangerous. Sleep-**deprived** people get into more car crashes. They get more diseases—from common colds to diabetes. And they get depressed more often.

Take the case of 17-year-old Randy Gardner. In 1964, he stayed awake for 11 days straight. The feat put him in the Guinness Book of World Records. But he paid for it. After a few days, he couldn't focus his eyes. Eventually, he started slurring his words, and he fell into a long **stupor**.

Experts say stunts like Randy's can be dangerous. In a 1983 study, scientists kept rats awake for days. After two and a half weeks, many of the rats died.

Chances are you're not going to try to follow Randy into the record books. But you may well get behind the wheel of a car after pulling an all-nighter. And that can be even more dangerous. Every year, 100,000 automobile accidents are linked to **drowsy** drivers. Those accidents cause 1,500 deaths. And half of them involve drivers aged 15 to 24. Almost one out of four teens admits having dozed off while driving. "It's not unlike driving drunk," Carskadon says. "When sleepy people get behind the wheel of a car, they're a danger to everyone."

So, how much sleep do you really need? If you're a teenager, the answer is: more than most people. Everyone has a kind of internal clock that controls their sleep patterns. The clock runs on a chemical called melatonin, which makes you sleepy. At night, your body starts making more **melatonin**. Your eyelids droop and it gets tough to stay awake. In the morning, your body slows down the melatonin flow. That makes it easier to wake up.

Scientists have recently found out that teenagers have a different sleep cycle than younger kids or adults. They need about 9.2 hours a night. That's about an hour more than most other people. Everyone is different, but the ideal night's sleep for most teens is midnight to 9 A.M.

In the past few years, some schools have started opening later. In 1996, a high school in Edina, Minnesota, pushed its opening time from 7:30 A.M. to 8:30 A.M. It seems to have worked. Absences are down and grades are up.

The facts are clear: Sleep is good. But most people still don't realize it. Teens and adults alike seem to think sleeping is a sign of laziness. Getting by on a few hours a night proves you're hard-working and strong. Just listen to Liz. "If I get more than six hours sleep a night, something's wrong," she says. "It means there's something else I should be doing."

Well, no. You should probably just close your eyes and go back to sleep.

Dream On

Have you ever wondered what those crazy dreams mean?

Something feels strange about math class today. You're about to take the final exam. But you forgot to study. What's more, you're sitting at your desk naked! The teacher is on his way over and suddenly—you wake up.

Some dreams are pretty common. Most people fall, fly, or get caught unprepared in their dreams. Wonder what those dreams are all about? Here are the basics.

What are dreams anyway?

Basically, they are a sign that your brain is working, even when you're asleep. Some researchers say they don't really mean anything. Others say the brain is working out problems from our waking lives.

So, what's the "Naked-in-Class Dream" trying to tell me?

Nudity in a dream usually means you feel vulnerable or scared about something. It may not be math, though. Dreams are often disguised, like poems. You have to dig to get the true meaning.

How about the one in which I'm unprepared for a test?

Chances are you're afraid of failing at something. You could be worried about meeting your girlfriend's or boyfriend's parents. Or maybe you're afraid you won't play well in the big game. Most likely, your brain is trying to tell you to stop worrying so much.

What about dreams in which someone's chasing me?

This one is the most common. About 80 percent of people surveyed say they've had one. You probably feel someone in your life is out to get you. Or you could be running from an issue that you don't want to face.

Is it weird to have dreams in which I'm falling? What about "flying" dreams?

Not at all. Falling can mean that you fear you're losing your grip. Something may be making you feel helpless. Flying is the exact opposite. In that dream, you feel totally secure and in control. It's one of the few dreams that is uplifting. Two-thirds of all dreams deal with unpleasant subjects. That's probably because they're helping us solve problems.

Don't Go for the Burn

Marissa Ruhl loves stretching out in the sun. She lets the warm rays cover her from head to toe. "I'm addicted to the sun," admits the 18-year-old from South Miami, Florida. "I can sit out in the sun from 11 A.M. to 5 P.M."

Does Marissa care about getting sunburned? Is she concerned about the sun's **ultraviolet (UV) rays** wrinkling her skin? Does she realize her body is a sitting duck for skin cancer?

Sort of. "I didn't wear sunscreen until my nose kept getting red and raw," Marissa says. "Now I put sunscreen on my face. But I don't put it on anywhere else."

Marissa is playing a dangerous game with the sun. And she's not the only one. Lots of teenagers say they don't regularly put sunscreen on their bodies. That's bad news because the sun will do 80 percent of its damage to your skin before you turn 18. The effects won't show up until later. But when they do, you'll know it. Too much sun will make your skin wrinkled. It will produce ugly brown spots. And worst of all, it can give you skin cancer.

At first glance, it just doesn't seem right. The sun can make you feel great. It helps fight off depression. And tans are supposed to make you look healthy.

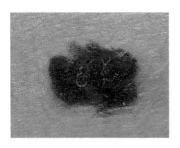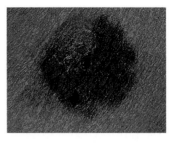

Melanoma, a deadly skin cancer, can begin as a small growth. See your doctor if you find any growths on your body that are asymmetrical, uneven in color, wider than $1/4$ inch, or have an irregular edge.

In fact, there's *nothing* healthy about a suntan. It's actually your skin's way of responding to an injury. When UV rays hit your skin, they attack the skin cells. To protect itself, your skin produces a brown chemical called **melanin**. The melanin makes you look nice and tan. But its main purpose is to block the rays that are making your skin sick.

Skin cancer is the most dangerous risk for sun worshippers. About one million Americans get it each year. Most kinds of skin cancer are easy to cure. **Melanoma** is not. More than 40,000 people a year end up with melanoma. Of those, nearly 8,000 die.

Melanoma is the most common kind of cancer in women aged 20 to 29. It can take as long as 10 or 20 years to develop. That means women in their twenties probably planted the seeds of their cancer while they were in their teens. It's a good idea to avoid getting a blistering sunburn. Just one can double your risk of getting melanoma.

Most beach bums won't die from cancer. But unprotected sunbathing will take its toll in other ways. When UV rays get into your skin, they attack **collagen** and elastin. These are proteins that keep your skin smooth and soft. In healthy skin, elastin looks like smooth, woven bundles. Too many UV rays make elastin look like cooked spaghetti. The skin above it ends up dry and wrinkled.

So, what are you supposed to do? Stay in the basement all summer?

Hardly. It's actually not that tough to protect yourself from the sun.

First of all, use sunscreen. Find one with an **SPF** (Sun Protection Factor) of 15 or higher. The number tells you how much of the sun's UV rays are getting screened out. The higher the number, the better the protection. SPF 15 means that you can stay in the sun 15 times longer than normal without getting burned. Using SPF 15 or higher can cut your risk of skin cancer by 78 percent.

It also helps to know when and why the sun does its worst damage. UV rays are at their peak between 10 A.M. and 2 P.M. Half the sun's daily dose is given out during those four hours. The sun is weaker during the winter, when it's lower in the sky. But you can still get burned—especially in the snow. Surfaces like snow, water, and concrete reflect the sun. They can actually send more UV rays your way. Don't be fooled by cloudy weather either. About 80 percent of the sun's rays can slip through the clouds.

Finally, you should know your own body. People with fair skin, blue eyes, and light-colored hair have a higher risk of getting skin cancer. If you burn easily, be careful. That's a sign that the sun is doing damage. Dark-skinned people have to be careful, too. They produce more melanin, which helps protect against the sun. But it doesn't ensure that they won't get skin cancer.

So, don't run from the sun. Just treat it with caution. Be wise and you won't get burned.

Got Sunblock?

Here's a sun-worshipper's guide
to the greasy stuff.

- Use SPF 15 or higher. That means you'll burn 15 times slower than you would with nothing on. Suppose you'd normally burn in 10 minutes. With SPF 15, you can stay out for 150 minutes (2 1/2 hours) before burning. Just remember, putting it on again *doesn't* give you another 2 1/2 hours.

- Slather it on. Use too little sunscreen and you can cut the SPF in half. You should use one ounce every time you put it on.

- Put it on early. Sunscreen takes 20 minutes to bind to the proteins in your skin. Before then it's not as effective.

- Put it on often. Sunscreen wears off every four hours. If you're swimming, it's gone after two hours.

- Put it on everywhere. Missing a patch of skin can be bad news. You think you're protected so you stay out too long. You end up with a blistering red blotch the shape of Texas.

- Take extra care if you're fair. If you're very light-skinned or have a history of skin cancer, be careful. Consider a sunscreen with titanium dioxide or zinc oxide. These block UV rays more effectively.

Test Your Solar IQ

How enlightened are you about the sun?

Take this quiz and see. You'll find some—but not all—of the answers in this chapter. Mark each of the statements below *true* or *false*. When you're finished check the answer key. Count how many questions you got right. Then check your score on page 64.

1. You don't need to wear sunscreen in the shade.

2. Tanning beds are a safe way to get a tan.

3. Getting a bad sunburn can double your risk of getting skin cancer.

4. The sun is less dangerous during the winter.

5. Sunscreen doesn't dissolve in water, so it lasts all day long.

6. Most skin cancer is not fatal.

7. If you have dark skin, you are protected from the sun.

8. If your father had skin cancer, you will get it too.

9. Clothes give you full protection from the sun.

10. If you get sunburned, you should drink liquids and use moisturizer.

Answers

1. False. Direct sun is the most dangerous. But shade doesn't protect you from reflected rays. If you're near concrete, water, snow, or sand, you can still get up to 85 percent of the sun's rays.

2. False. It's harder to burn in tanning beds. But they can still wrinkle your skin and cause cancer.

3. True. All you have to do is get one blistering sunburn. Your risk of developing a melanoma—the most dangerous kind of skin cancer—later in life will double.

4. True. UV rays are less direct because the sun is lower in the sky. But that doesn't mean you can't get hurt. You can still get a sunburn. Rays are particularly bad if there is snow on the ground to reflect the sun.

5. False. It doesn't matter what it says on the bottle. Put new sunscreen on every four hours. Make it every two hours if you're swimming.

6. True. One million Americans get skin cancer every year. Fewer than 8,000 of them die from it.

7. False. You are probably less likely to be damaged by UV rays than a fair-skinned person. But you still need to use sunscreen.

8. False. You are more likely to get skin cancer if your parents have had it. But you can lower your risk by being careful in the sun.

9. False. Most clothing will protect you well enough. But loosely woven shirts will let the sun in. A white T-shirt, for instance, has an SPF of 5 when dry. If it gets wet, the SPF drops to 1—and that's the same as having no protection at all.

10. True. Cool baths will help too. A first-degree sunburn should heal within a few days. If you get blisters plus a headache, chills, or a fever, you should see a doctor.

Your Score

8–10: Bravo. Your skin thanks you.

5–7: Not bad. A little more caution couldn't hurt.

1–4: You're going for the burn. Go for some sunscreen instead.

Glossary

aerobic exercise *(noun)* energetic exercise that strengthens the heart and improves breathing

antibiotic *(noun)* a drug that kills bacteria and is used to cure infections and diseases

artery *(noun)* one of the tubes that carries blood from the heart to all the other parts of the body

bacteria *(noun)* extremely small living things that exist all around and inside you. Many bacteria are useful, but some cause disease.

calcium *(noun)* a soft, silver-white chemical element found in teeth and bones

carbohydrates *(noun)* one of the substances in such foods as bread, rice, and potatoes that gives you energy

cholesterol *(noun)* a fatty substance that humans and animals need to digest food and produce certain vitamins and hormones. Too much cholesterol in the blood can increase the possibility of heart disease.

collagen *(noun)* a protein in your skin

congestion *(noun)* an area that is blocked up

deprived *(adjective)* prevented from having something

diabetes *(noun)* a disease in which there is too much sugar in the blood

drowsy *(adjective)* sleepy, tired

elastin *(noun)* a protein in your skin

glucose *(noun)* a natural sugar found in plants that gives energy to living things

immune system *(noun)* the system that protects your body from disease and infection

influenza *(noun)* an illness that is like a bad cold, with fever and muscle pains. It is caused by a virus. Most people call it "the flu" for short.

melanin *(noun)* a brown chemical produced by your skin when it's hit by UV rays

melanoma *(noun)* a kind of cancer

melatonin *(noun)* a chemical produced by your body that makes you sleepy

membrane *(noun)* a very thin layer of tissue or skin that lines or covers certain organs or cells

mineral *(noun)* a substance found in nature that is not an animal or a plant. Gold, salt, and copper are all minerals.

monounsaturated fat *(noun)* fat that comes from vegetable oils. It is thought to be healthier for you than other fats.

mucus *(noun)* a slimy fluid that coats and protects the inside of your mouth, nose, throat, and other breathing passages

nasal *(adjective)* having to do with your nose

nutrient *(noun)* something that is needed by people, animals, and plants to stay strong and healthy. Proteins, minerals, and vitamins are all nutrients.

osteoporosis *(noun)* a condition in which a person's bone mass decreases

pasteurized *(adjective)* heated to a temperature that is high enough to kill harmful bacteria

pathogen *(noun)* a germ that causes disease

perishable *(adjective)* likely to spoil or decay quickly

physical therapist *(noun)* someone who treats diseased or injured muscles and joints by physical means, such as exercise, massage, and heat

pneumonia *(noun)* a serious disease that causes the lungs to become inflamed and filled with a thick fluid that makes breathing difficult

polyunsaturated fat *(noun)* fat that comes from vegetable oils. It is thought to be healthier for you than other fats.

protein *(noun)* a substance found in all living plant and animal cells. Foods such as meat, cheese, eggs, beans, and fish are sources of protein.

pulse *(noun)* the beat of blood moving through a vein or artery

saturated fat *(noun)* fat that comes from meat, as well as from dairy products. Also, palm and coconut oils

SPF *(adjective)* abbreviation for Sun Protection Factor

stupor *(noun)* a dazed state

ultraviolet ray *(noun)* light that cannot be seen by the human eye. It is given off by the sun and causes the skin to get darker.

UV *(adjective)* abbreviation for ultraviolet

vaccine *(noun)* a substance, injected or swallowed, that protects a person from disease

vaporizer *(noun)* a machine that creates water vapor or steam

vitamin *(noun)* one of the substances in food that is necessary for good health